LIFESKILLS™ HANDBOOKS

Managing Money

Nan Bostick

and

Susan M. Freese

RECEIVED
APR 18 2012
By_____

21st CENTURY

HAYNER PUBLIC LIBRARY DISTRICT
ALTON, ILLINOIS

OVERDUES 10 PER DAY, MAXIMUM FINE
COST OF ITEM
ADDITIONAL $5.00 SERVICE CHARGE
APPLIED TO
LOST OR DAMAGED ITEMS

HAYNER PLD/ALTON SQUARE

SADDLEBACK
EDUCATIONAL PUBLISHING

SADDLEBACK
EDUCATIONAL PUBLISHING
www.sdlback.com

Copyright © 2012 by Saddleback Educational Publishing
All rights reserved. No part of this book may be reproduced in any form or by any
means, electronic or mechanical, including photocopying, recording, scanning, or by
any information storage and retrieval system, without the written permission of the
publisher. SADDLEBACK EDUCATIONAL PUBLISHING and any associated logos are
trademarks and/or registered trademarks of Saddleback Educational Publishing.

ISBN-13: 978-1-61651-659-8
ISBN-10: 1-61651-659-3
eBook: 978-1-61247-347-5

Printed in Guangzhou, China
1111/CA21101811

16 15 14 13 12   1 2 3 4 5

Y332.024
BOS

b19971692

Contents

Section 1	**Controlling Your Spending**	5
Chapter 1	Developing Thrifty Habits	8
Chapter 2	Balancing Wants and Needs	14
Chapter 3	Keeping Financial Records	20
Chapter 4	Common Financial Mistakes	26
Section 2	**Banking Basics**	33
Chapter 1	Choosing a Bank	36
Chapter 2	Checking Accounts and Check Registers	42
Chapter 3	Monthly Bank Statements	48
Chapter 4	Savings Accounts	54
Section 3	**Buy Now, Pay Later**	61
Chapter 1	Dangers of Debt	64
Chapter 2	Using Credit Cards	70
Chapter 3	Borrowing Money	76
Chapter 4	Installment Purchases	82
Section 4	**Improving Your Budgeting Skills**	89
Chapter 1	Your Goal: A Balanced Budget	92
Chapter 2	Keeping a Personal Expense Record	98
Chapter 3	Typical Budget Adjustments	104
Chapter 4	Handling Unexpected Expenses	110
Word List		116
Index		118

Controlling Your Spending

Controlling spending is hard for many people. Some people make bad spending choices over and over. Then, they never seem to have enough money for the things they need. Other people try to be careful. But they don't understand some basic ideas about smart spending. You can take control of your spending by correcting your bad habits and learning how to avoid costly mistakes.

It All Adds Up!

Erin was glad to get home! She'd had classes all morning and then worked an eight-hour shift at the store. Now, she was ready to relax. She'd have the apartment all to herself. Her roommate, Cassie, was working tonight.

But when Erin walked into the apartment, she immediately tensed up. The TV was blaring in the living room, and the lights were on all through the apartment. A nearly full can of soda was sitting on the kitchen counter. Next to it was an open container of takeout food from the deli.

"Cassie . . ." Erin muttered to herself, as she tossed the container into the wastebasket.

This wasn't the first time Erin had come home to a situation like this. Cassie was wasteful, in Erin's view. She didn't worry about what things cost. And she never planned how to spend what she earned. Last summer, she'd even bought a new car without giving it much thought.

Keeping up with the payments on that car was hard for Cassie. She also had some credit card bills to pay. More and more, she struggled to pay her share of the rent and utilities. Erin worried that soon, Cassie wouldn't have enough money. And then Erin would get stuck paying more than her share!

Erin didn't consider herself a financial genius. But she had common sense about spending money. She knew that it was easy to form bad habits. She also knew that little things add up. And she knew that she couldn't have everything she wanted.

She wished Cassie knew some of these things too.

CHAPTER **1**

Developing Thrifty Habits

A *habit* is something you do all the time without really thinking about it. Some habits are good, but others are bad.

Do you have any bad habits when it comes to money? Do you waste money? If so, how much do you think you could save by correcting your bad spending habits?

Let's say that on average, you spend $3 a day drinking energy drinks or soda. To be ***thrifty***, you could start drinking tap water instead. In five days, you'd have an extra $15. And in a year, you'd be $1,095 richer!

> **Thrifty**
> Careful and smart with money.

8

Making Simple Changes

Clearly, having thrifty habits saves money. Making even simple changes, like turning off the lights, can add up to big savings. And once you get started, it becomes easy to think of new ways to save. But resisting the temptation to spend can be very hard.

In today's world, we're hit over and over again with clever and attractive **marketing schemes**. They're designed to convince us to spend our money on things we don't need and maybe can't even afford. How many advertisements, or ads, have you seen lately that suggest you go into debt to purchase something?

Sometimes, your friends encourage your bad spending habits. Do you ever feel you must buy things to keep up with your friends? If so, you're feeling peer pressure. Giving in to peer pressure can be very expensive.

Marketing

The business of advertising and selling products and services.

Scheme

A plan or system, sometimes involving a secret or trick.

Learning to Be Frugal

It isn't easy to resist peer pressure. Most people want to do what everyone else does or to have what everyone else has. You need to convince yourself that it's important to be *frugal*.

Some people tighten their spending to save money for something special, such as college tuition. Others develop thrifty habits to avoid going into debt. They also know it's important to have money available for both emergencies and unexpected opportunities.

Think of reasons that could convince you to save money and to stop buying things you don't need. What could you go without in your life?

Frugal
Careful with money to the point of going without things.

Tips for Saving Money

Some wasteful habits are easy to change. Others are more difficult to correct and may take time and effort.

Read the following money-saving tips. Which of these suggestions would help you become more thrifty?

→ Turn off lights, TVs, and radios whenever you leave home.

→ Avoid buying snack foods from vending machines. Pack your own snacks and carry them with you.

→ Stop spending money on candy and junk food.

→ Walk or ride a bike instead of paying for gas or bus fare.

→ Don't smoke. And if you already do, give it up.

→ Pack your own lunch for school or work instead of buying it.

→ When you shop, take just enough cash to buy the things you need. Leave your checkbook and debit and credit cards at home.

Tips for Resisting Peer Pressure

- **Choose friends who influence you in good ways, not bad ways.** True friends will respect your values and decisions.

- **Avoid activities that involve things you don't want to do.** Think in advance about what might be involved, and decide whether you want to participate.

- **Make decisions that fit your values, and follow through with them.** Don't make decisions or change your mind based on other people's values and expectations.

- **Consider the possible consequences of your behavior.** Could you get in trouble? Could you get hurt or harm your health?

- **Practice ways to say "no."** Tell the truth or make up an excuse for not getting involved in something.

Average Living Expenses

Of course, there are some things in life we have to pay for, such as food, housing, clothing, and transportation. These costs are often called *living expenses*. The average person's living expenses total $32,650 a year. Here's the breakdown of expenses:

1. **Food:** $6,372
2. **Housing:** $16,895
3. **Clothing:** $1,725
4. **Transportation:** $7,658

CHAPTER 2

Balancing Wants and Needs

Everybody needs to eat. But do you *need* to eat at a restaurant? Probably not. You may *like* and *want* to do that. But to save money, you could prepare your own food and eat at home.

Setting Priorities

When you purchase things such as movie tickets and restaurant meals, you're spending money on things you *want*. It's fine to buy things you want, of course—if you can afford them.

But first, you should make sure you have enough money to pay for your needs. Your *needs* are your necessary expenses. They include things you can't do without, such as food, water, shelter, and electricity. The things you need must be your **priorities**.

Priorities
Things of greatest importance.

[FACT]

Entertainment Costs
The average American spends 5.5% of his or her yearly income on entertainment. That comes to about $2,693 per year, on average. These costs include going to movies, concerts, ball games, and other events. They also include monthly utilities, such as cable or satellite television. And for many Americans, a growing entertainment expense is service plans for cell phones, video games, and other technological devices. Some people spend $1,000 a year alone on these kinds of service plans.

Identifying Wants versus Needs

Can you tell the difference between *wants* and *needs*? Doing so is important if you want to manage your money wisely.

Try these two suggestions for identifying wants versus needs:

1. Think about why you want to buy an item. Try to come up with at least three good reasons for making the purchase. If you can't, the item is probably something you *want*, not something you *need*.

2. Ask yourself "What will happen if I *don't* buy this item?" For instance, suppose you're thinking about buying a new bedspread.

Shopping Checklist

Before you head to the mall, think about what you want to buy and why you want to buy it. Ask yourself these questions:

☐ Why am I going shopping? Do I just want to shop around, or do I really need something?

☐ If I need something, why do I think I need it? Can I prove that I need it?

☐ If I just want to shop around, can I actually do that? Can I look without buying?

☐ Have I paid all of my bills? Do I have other needs to pay for or to save for?

☐ If I plan to buy, am I willing to go to several stores and look for the best price?

If you don't buy it, nothing will probably happen. Even if your old bedspread is completely worn out, you don't have to replace it. You could go without. This means the bedspread is a *want*. But what about paying your electric bill? If you fail to make the payment, your service will be **disconnected**. You won't have electricity anymore, which would be a huge problem. This means paying the electric bill is a *need*.

Disconnected
Shut off or discontinued.

The Pleasure of Purchasing

Why do we like to shop? There's a chemical in our brains called *dopamine*. It's called the "feel good" chemical, because it's related to pleasure. When dopamine is released into our bodies, we feel good. And when something makes us feel good, we usually want to do it again and again.

Seeing an item we want in the store excites the brain. The more we want the item, the more excited the brain gets. Buying the item satisfies that want, and the brain releases dopamine. The more we buy, the more shopping brings us pleasure.

Sometimes, what you want and what you need are the same. For example, if you've outgrown or worn out your winter coat, you want *and* need to replace it. You can still try to save money, though. You might shop for a coat at a discount clothing outlet, or you might look for a bargain at a local thrift store.

Coming Up Short

Sam hasn't learned to tell the difference between wants and needs. And now, his rent is due! He's $55 short, which means he's spent too much on wants.

Read the following list of Sam's expenses this week. Which items are *wants*, not *needs*?

DVD and
video game rentals $11.98
Electricity bill $45.90
Phone bill $25.90
New soccer ball $33.98
Energy drinks $5.09
Groceries $26.50
Laundry $6.00
Ice-cream sundae $3.95
Transportation $35.20

Which items did you identify as *wants*? How much did Sam spend on these items?

Of the expenses on Sam's list, these items are *wants*: DVD and game rentals, new soccer ball, energy drinks, ice-cream sundae. As it turns out, they add up to $55, which is exactly how much more Sam needs to pay his rent.

A Simple Plan

A simple plan for managing your money is to split your earnings three ways:

1. **50% for needs:** expenses that must be paid, including payments on debts.

2. **30% for wants:** expenses that could be put off without any serious consequences.

3. **20% for savings:** a fund to cover unexpected expenses.

20%
Savings

30%
Wants

50%
Needs

CHAPTER **3**

Keeping Financial Records

It's easy to spend money. But it can be hard to keep track of how much you spend.

In keeping track of your spending, don't rely on your memory alone. Financial advisors suggest keeping good financial records.

What Are Financial Records?

A *financial record* is any **document** that **verifies** the amount of money you earn, spend, or save. All the documents discussed in the following section are types of financial records.

Document

A written explanation or record. Many documents are used to provide proof of something.

Verify

To prove that something is accurate or true.

20

Types of Financial Records

Expense Report

An *expense report* is a detailed list of everything you spend. People who travel for their jobs often keep expense reports to show costs of transportation, meals, hotels, and so on.

If you'd like to track your spending habits, try keeping an expense report. Becoming aware of your spending habits will help you to identify waste.

Budget

A *budget* is a written plan for managing money. It should include how much you expect to earn and how much you expect to spend.

Preparing and sticking to a budget makes sense. It will help keep you out of debt and find new ways to save money.

Receipts

Receipts are records of purchases. You usually get a receipt when you buy something. This slip of paper shows *when*, *where*, and *what* you paid for.

Always get a dated receipt when you buy something, especially when you pay with cash. Also, keep your receipts well organized. Then, you'll be able to find a receipt easily when you need it.

Receipts are needed or useful in these situations:

→ To prove you paid a bill on time

→ To return something you've purchased

→ To prove that you loaned money to someone

→ To track daily expenses or plan a budget

Bank Records

Banking involves several kinds of financial records. If you have a bank account, you should keep track of these records:

→ **Deposit slips:** These are records of your deposits, or times you put money into your account. Each deposit slip proves how much money you added, along with when and where you made the deposit.

→ **Withdrawal slips:** These are records of your withdrawals, or times you took money out of your account. Each withdrawal slip proves not only how much you took out but when and where.

→ **Register:** The register is your personal record of all the transactions in your account. It lists deposits and withdrawals, checks, service charges, and so on. Recording these activities allows you to keep track of how much money is in the account. That amount is called the *balance*.

Recordkeeping and the IRS

The Internal Revenue Service (IRS) sometimes requires taxpayers to provide financial records. If the IRS ever questions information on your tax return, you'll have to provide the financial records to back up what you've reported. The IRS suggests you keep the following yearly financial records for six years:

- Bank statements
- Deposit slips and withdrawal slips
- Cancelled checks (checks that have been paid)
- Records of income (such as W-2 and 1099 forms)
- Receipts of major items sold for cash (such as cars or equipment)
- Receipts of major expenses (such as house payments and medical bills)
- Receipts of money and items donated to churches and charities

Tips for Organizing Your Bills and Records

- Keep all bills and financial records in the same place, such as a desk or file cabinet.
- Set up a recordkeeping system and then use it.
- Color-code materials based on their importance. For instance, put bills that need immediate payment in a red folder.
- Keep items that don't need immediate attention separate from items that do.
- Pay your bills online as much as possible. Print out receipts or other proof of having made payment.

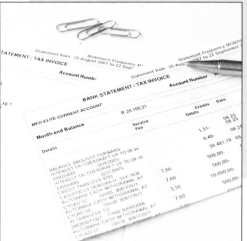

- Keep a calendar for paying bills. Write down when you make each payment.
- Use a paper shredder to get rid of documents you don't need to keep.

Transaction

An act of doing business. For a bank account, transactions include all of the acts of adding or taking out money.

Safe Storage of Financial Records

- **Lock box:** Storing records in a locked metal box will protect them from being stolen. Lock boxes aren't usually fireproof, though.

- **File cabinet:** Using a file cabinet is great way to keep files organized. Some file cabinets can be locked for security. File cabinets aren't usually fireproof.

- **Safe:** Having a safe is the best way to protect records at home. Make sure the safe is fireproof, however.

- **Safe deposit box:** Having a safe deposit box is the most secure way to store financial records. You rent this kind of box at your bank, usually for a small fee each year.

→ **Statement:** The statement is the report about your account you receive from the bank each month. It shows all the *transactions* for the month, plus the current balance. You should always check the statement against the register and other financial records you keep. Make sure you and the bank agree on how much money you have.

Storing Financial Records

Be sure to keep your financial records in a safe place. Many times, these documents contain information you want to keep private. Also, some financial records are difficult to replace, if lost or damaged.

CHAPTER 4

Common Financial Mistakes

Being ***careless*** with money can cost you more than you think. And over time, purchasing mistakes can turn into bad spending habits.

Careless

Not paying attention or showing concern.

Unit pricing

How much 1 unit of something costs. For example, milk is sold in several different sizes of containers: half-pint, pint, quart, half-gallon, and gallon. Knowing the unit price of 1 cup of milk, as it's sold in all these different sizes, will help you decide which size is the best buy. Usually, the larger the size or quantity, the lower the unit price.

Shopping Mistakes

→ Buying things without first looking for better prices elsewhere.

→ Not using **unit pricing** to determine the best buys.

→ Not checking or saving sales receipts.

→ Failing to return or exchange unsatisfactory purchases.

→ Buying unneeded things on **impulse.**

→ Buying unneeded items because they're on sale.

→ Driving a long distance to save a small amount of money.

Impulse
A strong desire or sudden urge.

→ Buying poorly made products just because they're low in price.

→ Buying things you can't afford to keep up with your friends.

→ Carrying more cash than needed when shopping.

→ Not being aware of the costs of using credit cards.

Tips for Shopping at Warehouse Retailers

Many people save money by shopping at warehouse retailers, such as Sam's Club and Costco. These kinds of stores offer low prices for buying items in *bulk*, or large quantities.

But buying in bulk doesn't always provide the best deal. Follow these tips to spend wisely at warehouse retailers:

- Know how much items usually cost. Some-times, grocery stores offer the same or lower prices and let you buy in smaller amounts.

- Don't buy more of something than you'll be able to use. In particular, don't buy items that will go bad before you can use them.

- If you're single or have a small household, shop with a friend. Split up items bought in bulk, and split the cost, as well.

- Pay attention to sales. Many items can be stored for later use, so buy them in bulk while they're on sale.

What Is Compulsive Shopping?

As many as 6 out of 100 Americans are *compulsive shoppers*. These individuals are driven to buy things and often can't control their behavior.

Here are the signs of compulsive shopping:

- Prefer to shop alone
- Often shop for unneeded items
- Have trouble not thinking about shopping and buying
- Struggle with self-control when shopping
- Have financial problems because of shopping
- Have problems at work, school, or home because of shopping
- Hide or don't use items that have been purchased
- Feel depressed or upset after buying something

If you or someone you know may be a compulsive shopper, talk to your doctor about getting help.

Payment Mistakes

→ Sending cash in the mail.

→ Making only a small payment on a debt if you can afford to pay it off completely.

→ Paying bills late or skipping payments.

→ Ignoring the costly fines for skipped or late payments.

→ Ignoring calls about skipped or late payments.

Banking Mistakes

→ Not shopping around for the best services.

→ Not keeping your bank register up to date.

→ Not reviewing your monthly bank statement and matching it up against your register.

→ Failing to ask for a correction when the bank has made an error.

→ Paying penalties for spending more money than is in the account or not keeping a required balance.

→ Not double-checking your addition and subtraction in your bank register.

→ Not keeping records of deposits and withdrawals.

→ Not setting up a savings account and making regular, small deposits.

How to Handle Creditors

Creditors are businesses you owe money to, such as banks and credit card companies. If you've missed payments, you'll likely get calls from these businesses. They have the right to ask when you expect to pay them.

Don't ignore these calls! Instead, follow these tips for talking to creditors:

1. Make sure the information they provide about what you owe is correct.

2. Answer and return phone calls. Refusing to talk to creditors will only delay reaching a solution. And you'll get even more calls!

3. Be honest. Admit your financial situation, and suggest working out a plan for payment.

4. Be calm and polite. Don't let your bad behavior make the creditor not want to work with you.

5. Follow through on your promises. If you say you'll make a payment but then can't, call the creditor immediately to explain.

6. Don't accept rude or threatening treatment by a creditor. Ask to speak to his or her manager.

Banking Basics

Most people deal with banks on a regular basis. They deposit their paychecks, put money into savings, pay their bills, and withdraw cash. But in fact, most people don't really think about banking. You should know what services your bank offers and what those services cost you and earn you. Choosing a bank is an important part of managing your money.

Making Ends Meet

It was near the end of the month, and Tyler was feeling a little short of cash. He'd get paid on Friday and would have enough to cover the next month's rent. But in the meantime, he wanted to make sure he didn't overspend.

Tyler was fairly sure he had about $150 left in his checking account. He kept track of his spending and usually had a good idea of how much money he had in the bank. But when he went online to review his account, he saw he had only $105. How could that be?

Feeling worried, Tyler took a close look at his checking account. He saw several charges for bank fees. One was for a review of his account. He knew he paid that every month. He wasn't sure why, though.

Several other fees were for withdrawing money at ATM machines. In some cases, Tyler was being charged two fees for a single withdrawal. He remembered withdrawing the money when he was out with his friends. But at the time, he hadn't realized the fees he'd have to pay.

"Thank goodness I'm not overdrawn!" Tyler thought. Spending more than he had in the account would cost even more fees. His bank charged an overdraft fee. It also charged another fee for each check that couldn't be paid. Tyler had been overdrawn once, and it had cost him almost $100 in fees.

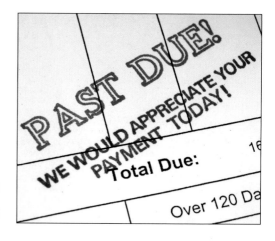

Tyler didn't want that to happen again. So, he took $100 from his savings account and put it into his checking account. He knew that if he transferred the money himself, he wouldn't have to pay a fee. He'd have to pay more attention to all these fees!

CHAPTER **1**

Choosing a Bank

Do you keep all your money hidden in your house? Do you cash your paycheck and lose track of how much money you have? Do you feel unsafe when you're carrying too much cash or have too much cash at home? Do you spend money without even thinking about it?

Did you answer "yes" to any of these questions? Then it's time to consider keeping your money in a bank account.

Why Use a Bank?

Keeping your money in a bank makes sense for all these reasons:

→ Keeping your money in a bank will prevent it from being lost or stolen.

→ Banks provide monthly statements, which will help you manage your money.

→ It's convenient to have your paycheck deposited directly into your account.

→ It's convenient to write checks and pay bills online.

→ Putting money into savings earns money through paid *interest*.

→ Getting a loan is usually easier for someone who has a bank account.

Interest

The fee paid for using money. Banks *pay interest* to people who put money in savings accounts, because banks use this money to make loans. Banks *charge interest* to people who get loans.

[FACT]

Banks During the Great Depression

In the 1930s, many US banks failed during a period of economic hardship known as the Great Depression. The Depression started with the stock market crash of 1929. People got worried about the economy and began taking money out of their banks. This left many banks with no money for making loans.

When banks couldn't make loans, they stopped earning money too. Banks lost even more money when many of the loans they had made weren't paid back. A lot of people lost their jobs during the Depression and couldn't pay back what they owed.

By 1933, 11,000 of the nation's 25,000 banks had closed. Americans lost millions of dollars when their banks failed.

Finding the Right Bank

You should shop around for a bank, like you do when you make an important purchase. Compare the different services banks offer and what kinds of fees they charge. Choose the bank that provides the services you need for the lowest fees.

Kinds of Banks

Look into these different kinds of banks:

→ **Commercial banks:** Commercial banks offer the services most people need, such as everyday banking transactions and making loans. Most commercial banks have ***branch*** offices in many cities and towns. Most of these banks welcome people with small amounts of money.

→ **Savings banks:** Savings banks often offer the best deals to attract new customers. Some of these banks are small, while others have many branches.

→ **Credit unions:** Credit unions have membership requirements. You may need to belong to an employee or professional organization to join. Often, credit unions charge the lowest fees of all. Many are only local and have only a few branches.

Branch

An individual office or location of a larger company or organization.

Kinds of Accounts

There are basically two kinds of bank accounts:

→ **Savings account:** This type of account is used mainly to hold money. Opening the account is usually free, but some banks require keeping a certain amount in the account. A savings account usually earns interest. The rate of interest depends on how much money is on deposit and how long it will be held without any withdrawals.

→ **Checking account:** This type of account allows writing checks against the money held on deposit. Opening the account is usually free. However, most banks charge fees for providing checks and other services. Some checking accounts earn a low rate of interest.

Bank Services and Fees

Also consider the services banks offer and what they charge for those services:

→ Open a range of hours, including evenings and Saturdays.

→ Have many branches in convenient locations.

→ Have ATMs (Automated Teller Machines) in convenient locations and charge no fees or low fees for using them.

→ Charge no fees or low fees for banking online, having checks printed or getting traveler's checks.

→ Have 24-hour online or over-the-phone help with banking problems and questions.

Banking Protection Today

As a result of banks failing during the Great Depression, the US government now guarantees people won't lose their money if their bank fails. On January 1, 1934, the Federal Deposit Insurance Corporation (FDIC) was created. It protects account holders who have up to $250,000 on deposit. (That includes money in their checking and savings accounts combined.)

Banks today are members of the FDIC. Seeing an FDIC sign at your bank tells you that your money is safe. If your bank failed, you would get paid the amount you had on deposit by the FDIC. Since the FDIC was created, no one has lost money because of a failed bank.

Banking Safety

Modern banking is convenient and safe but involves some risks. Avoid situations that may put you in danger or draw you into a *scam*:

→ Use ATMs with caution. Don't use an ATM if anyone is standing nearby. In particular, make sure no one can see you enter your PIN number. And don't count the money you withdraw where others can watch you.

Scam

A dishonest scheme or trick.

Costs of Bank Services

Most banks charge fees for providing services to account holders. And unless you have a lot of money in your account, you'll likely pay for these services.

Most banks open accounts for free, such as savings and checking. But they may charge you fees for making transactions, such as transferring money and cashing checks. Banks may also charge you a fee for not keeping a required balance on deposit. Most banks also charge a monthly service fee for each account.

Banks usually offer free services at the ATMs they operate. You can deposit or withdraw money at these ATMs free of charge. But if you use another bank's ATM, you'll usually have to pay one or more fees.

→ Never tell anyone your ATM or your online user name and password. Also don't write down this information and carry it in your wallet or purse.

→ Be aware of online and telephone scams. Your bank will never e-mail or call you asking for your account number, password, or other private information. This kind of scam is called *phishing*.

CHAPTER **2**

Checking Accounts and Check Registers

It's never safe to send cash in the mail. Why? It could easily get lost or stolen. And if it were lost or stolen, you'd have no way to prove that you sent the money.

It's smarter and safer to put your money in a checking account. Using the money you have deposited in your account, you can write and mail checks. You can also set up *automatic* payments or make payments online for expenses such as utilities. You can also use a debit card linked to your account to make purchases.

Each month, the bank will send you a statement of your checking account. It will show all the deposits you made that month. It will also show all the checks you wrote and the payments or purchases you made. You can use your bank statement as proof of these payments.

Automatic

Happening on its own, without outside control or action.

Writing a Check

When you open a checking account, you'll receive a box of numbered checks. The checks are ***personalized*** and printed with your name, address, and account number.

Personalized

Created for or provided for a specific person.

What Is a Debit Card?

Think of a debit card as a substitute or replacement for carrying cash or using checks. When you use a debit card, money is taken directly from your bank account. It's like a credit card except that you're spending your own money, not borrowing money. You won't be charged interest, but you may pay a service fee to use a debit card.

Using a debit card can help you control your spending. You can't spend more money than you have in your account. Also, when you use a debit card, all your purchases will be listed on your monthly bank statement. This, too, can help you track expenses.

Look for all of this information on your own checks:

Account holder name, address, and phone number →

Amount of check written in words →

Name of person or company being paid →

Date of check →

Check number →

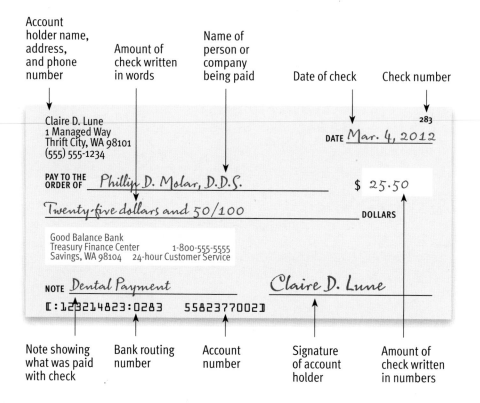

Claire D. Lune
1 Managed Way
Thrift City, WA 98101
(555) 555-1234

283

DATE *Mar. 4, 2012*

PAY TO THE ORDER OF *Phillip D. Molar, D.D.S.* $ 25.50

Twenty-five dollars and 50/100   DOLLARS

Good Balance Bank
Treasury Finance Center   1-800-555-5555
Savings, WA 98104   24-hour Customer Service

NOTE *Dental Payment*   *Claire D. Lune*

⑆:123214823:0283   5582377002⑈

Note showing what was paid with check

Bank routing number

Account number

Signature of account holder

Amount of check written in numbers

Using the Check Register

A *register* will come with your checks. It's a small booklet filled with pages of blank charts. Use it to record every transaction you make with your checking account. Then figure out your new balance, and record that too.

What transactions do you need to record? Write down each of the following:

→ Deposits made

→ Checks written

→ Cash withdrawn

→ Debit card charges

→ Automatic and online payments

When you make a deposit, *add the amount* to your balance. When you write a check, withdraw cash, use your debit card, or make an automatic or online payment, *subtract that amount* from your balance.

Be sure to subtract all bank service charges too. If you don't, you may think you have more money in the bank than you actually do.

And if your checking account earns interest, add that amount to the balance.

NUMBER OR CODE	DATE	TRANSACTION DESCRIPTION	PAYMENT AMOUNT	✓	FEE	DEPOSIT AMOUNT	$ BALANCE
			$			$	

Getting Overdrawn and "Bouncing" Checks

You must always keep enough money in your checking account to cover the checks you write, the debit card purchases you make, the bills you pay online or as automatic charges, and the service fees you pay. Otherwise, you'll get *overdrawn*. That means you've taken out more than you've deposited into the account. Banks charge high service fees for getting over-drawn.

If your account is over-drawn, your checks won't usually be **honored**. The bank will return them unpaid to the people and companies you wrote them to. Returned checks are sometimes stamped NSF, which stands for "**nonsufficient** funds." These checks are also called "bounced checks" or "bad checks."

Honored
Treated as having value, like money.

Nonsufficient
Not enough.

If you get overdrawn, the bank won't likely make automatic payments or online payments either. And if you try to use your debit card, you'll probably be turned down.

Having checks returned and payments refused results in additional service charges. Many banks charge $30 or more *per item* returned or refused. And of course, you still have to make the payments to the people and companies you owe money. Many companies charge their own service fees for returned checks and refused payments.

Overdraft Protection

Some checking accounts provide a service called *overdraft protection*. If you have this service, your bank will pay checks that are written and charges that are made when there's not enough money in your account. You won't "bounce" checks or get charged overdraft fees.

The money to cover your checks and payments will come from another account that's linked to your checking account:

- **That account might be your savings account, which contains your money.** The bank may charge you a service fee for moving money from your savings account into your checking account. If you transfer the money yourself, you won't likely pay a fee.

- **That account might be a line of credit, which is borrowed money.** Your bank will let you borrow up to a certain amount—perhaps $1,000. But like any loan, that money has to be paid back over time. Also, you'll be charged interest and fees for borrowing it.

CHAPTER **3**

Monthly Bank Statements

When you have a checking account, you'll record all the account transactions in the register. You'll also keep track of your balance there. That way, you'll know how much money you have in the account at any time.

For your checking account, you'll also receive a monthly statement from the bank. It will either come in the mail or be provided to you online. The bank statement will show all the account transactions for the past month, as your bank has recorded them. Likewise, the statement will show the month-ending balance, or the amount of money your bank says you have.

Every month, it's important to compare the bank statement with your checkbook register. This is called *reconciling* your checking account. Reconciling your account can help you avoid getting overdrawn.

> **Reconcile**
> To make the same or bring into agreement.

Reconciling Your Checking Account

To reconcile your checking account, compare the transactions in your register and your bank statement. Match them up, transaction by transaction.

In your checkbook register, look for a narrow column with a checkmark (✔) above it. Use this column to check off each transaction that

you've matched between the register and the statement. For instance, mark all the checks you recorded in the register that are shown as *cancelled* in the bank statement. But don't mark any checks the statement shows as *outstanding*. Likewise, match up other kinds of payments, plus all the deposits.

If you work through your register and statement this way, you should be able to successfully reconcile the two. You'll know you've been successful if you come up with the same final balance in both places. If you don't get the same balance, there's an error somewhere.

Cancelled check

A check that's been paid by the bank. Banks may send back cancelled checks to the person who wrote them or provide copies online, if needed.

Outstanding check

A check that hasn't yet been paid by the bank. A check that remains outstanding for more than a month may be lost. You should call the bank to stop payment on such a check.

Reconciling Jose's Checking Account

Take a look at Jose's bank statement:

Valley View Bank

Account Number: 12345678

Statement of Account
Statement Period
From: March 1, 2012
To: March 31, 2012

Jose Morales
1 Financial Way
Saverstown, CA 90046

Last Statement: February 28, 2012

Beginning Balance	Total Withdrawals	Total Deposits	Ending Balance
$75.36	$263.48	$300.00	$111.88

Date	Withdrawals	Deposits	Transaction Description
03/03		150.00	Customer Deposit
03/09	40.00		ATM Withdrawal
03/09	1.50		ATM Fee
03/15		150.00	Customer Deposit
03/31	6.50		Monthly Account Fee

Date	Check Number	Amount
03/07	403	135.00
03/09	404	69.50
03/24	405	10.98

Now look at Jose's checkbook register:

NUMBER OR CODE	DATE	TRANSACTION DESCRIPTION	PAYMENT AMOUNT	✓	FEE	DEPOSIT AMOUNT	$ BALANCE 75.36
ATM	3/3	Paycheck book store job	$ 0.00	✔		$150.00	225.36
ATM	3/3	Cash	40.00	✔			
		ATM fee	1.50	✔			183.86
403	3/7	Mom for room & board	135.00	✔			48.86
ATM	3/15	Paycheck book store job		✔		150.00	198.86
404	3/9	Campus Store textbooks	69.50	✔			129.36
405	3/24	Joe's Cafe Lunch with Bud	10.98	✔			118.38

At the end of the month, Jose thought he had $118.38 left in his account. That's what he recorded in his checkbook register. But on the bank statement, the Ending Balance was $111.88, or $6.50 less. Can you guess why?

To reconcile his account, Jose carefully compared his checkbook register with the bank statement. That's how he determined that he'd forgotten about the bank's $6.50 monthly service fee!

To correct this error, Jose recorded the $6.50 fee in his register. Then he subtracted that amount from $118.38. Doing so gave him a new balance of $111.88.

With this change, the final balance in Jose's register matched the final balance on the bank statement. His checking account was successfully reconciled!

Using Checkbook Software

Reconciling your checking account is a lot easier when you use checkbook software. The software creates an electronic checkbook register. You still have to enter all the transactions, but the math is all done for you!

Follow these tips for using checkbook software:

- Keep up with making entries. Enter transactions daily, if possible.
- Set up recurring payments, which you make every month.
- Tag the transactions according to type, like "Groceries" or "Gas."
- Set up automatic payments and deposits, which will be recorded every month.
- Print out the register every month after you've reconciled the account. Also back up the file on your computer.

Online Bank Statements

Today, many banks provide bank statements online or via the mail. You may be asked to choose one or the other method when setting up an account. Cancelled checks, deposit and withdrawal slips, and other records may also be provided online, if you choose that option. And you may be able to get a single statement or statements up to a year old.

Providing statements online saves banks huge costs in printing and mailing statements. And it saves you from having to file and organize months of financial records. If you get your statements online, you can always print them out.

Tips for Using Online Banking Services

- **Decide what services you need.** A range of services is available. Examples include automatic bill paying, money transfers, and automatic paycheck deposits.

- **Check the fees.** Some online services include fees. Make sure to budget for these fees so you don't get overdrawn.

- **Keep track of funds.** If you set up automatic payments, make sure you always have enough money in your account to cover them. Getting overdrawn will result in service fees from your bank and the company expecting payment.

- **Keep your login information private.** Choose a user name and password you will remember. But keep the information in a safe place that only you know.

CHAPTER **4**

Savings Accounts

If you're saving for something special, you should open a savings account. You'll be more likely to set aside the money you need. Plus, the bank will pay you interest for keeping your money on deposit.

[FACT]

Guidelines for Saving

- **Set up a savings account.** Shop around for the best interest rate and services.

- **Put away 10% of your income.** If you can't put aside 10%, then save what you can. But make sure to do it every month.

- **Think of the amount you save each month as an expense.** If you put money into savings on a regular basis, it will soon become a habit.

- **Have the money taken from your paycheck and deposited into your savings account.** Setting up automatic transactions will ensure you save a certain amount from every check.

- **Look carefully at your expenses.** Cutting back on monthly expenses will free up more money to put into savings.

Saving for Your Future

Most financial advisors point out the importance of starting to save money at a young age. Starting young develops good financial habits. In addition, because savings accounts earn interest, saving from a young age helps build up a nice sum of money. That money might be used for college or another expense later in life.

Suppose you start putting $30 a month into a savings account when you're 5 years old. The interest rate paid on the account is 1.16% a year. By the time you're 18, you will have saved just over $5,000. By the time you're 40, you'll have saved $15,515. And by the time you're 65, you'll have saved $31,128. All it took was saving $1 a day!

Earning Interest

The amount of interest you earn is a certain percentage of your account balance. The percentage is called the *interest rate*. To figure out how much interest you'll earn, multiply the balance by the percentage. In most cases, that's how much interest you'll earn in a year.

Suppose you put $500 in a savings account paying a yearly interest rate of 3%. Multiply $500 by 0.03 (which is another way to write 3%). The answer is $15. That's how much interest you'll earn for keeping $500 in your account for a year. (In fact, most banks pay interest daily, not yearly, so you'll probably earn a little more than $15.)

Interest rates vary from bank to bank, so shop around!

Types of Savings Accounts

There are several different kinds of savings accounts, and they pay different rates of interest. Check out all your options before deciding which kind of account is best for you:

	Type of Account			
	Regular Savings	**Starter**	**Money Market**	**Certificate of Deposit (CD)**
Description	Easy access to funds. Good for short-term goals or creating an emergency fund.	Great choice for students ages 8 to 18. Works like a regular savings account but has no bank fees.	High earnings with limited check writing allowed.	Guaranteed high interest for long-term savers.
Minimum Opening Deposit/Term	$50/None	$5/None	$2,500/None	$1,000/From 3 to 60 months
Interest Paid*	Variable rate	Variable rate	Variable rate	Fixed rate
Service Fees Charged	Small fee per month if balance falls below minimum required.	Not until individual is 18 years old.	Small fee per month if balance falls below minimum required.	None.
Access to Funds	Unlimited deposits and withdrawals. Use of ATM card. Available for overdraft protection	Unlimited deposits and withdrawals. Use of ATM card.	Can write a few checks a month (usually three). Unlimited deposits. Use of ATM card. Available for overdraft protection.	Fee charged for early withdrawals. No additional deposits.

* Rates are dependant on the economy and change frequently

Terms to Know

Access to funds: Refers to how often and how easily you can make deposits to and withdrawals from your account.

Fixed rate: The interest rate is set at a specific percentage and guaranteed not to change.

Minimum opening deposit: The smallest amount of money that can be used to open an account.

Overdraft protection: Banks sometimes link people's savings accounts and checking accounts. That makes the money in a savings account available to cover payments made in the checking account, if the account gets overdrawn. Having overdraft protection prevents you from paying high overdraft fees.

Term: The time period required. For instance, for a CD, a term of up to five years may be required.

Variable rate: The interest rate may change. For instance, it may be 3% when you open the account but fall to 1% the following month.

Access	**Minimum**	**Variable**
Right of use or entry.	The least possible or acceptable amount.	Able to change or be corrected.

Saving Trends among Americans

Financial advisors tell people to save at least 10% of their income. Saving 12% to 15% is believed to be ideal. Yet today, the average American saves just 6% of his or her income. Only 41% of Americans save money on a regular basis, and only 40% are saving for retirement. Worst of all, 43% of Americans spend more than they earn.

Americans saved the most money during World War II. At that time, the average American saved 26% of his or her income.

Average Americans' Savings, today

Average Americans' Savings, WWII

Americans Saving Regularly

Americans Saving for Retirement

Spending More Than They Earn

| 0 | 10 | 20 | 30 | 40 | 50 | 60 | 70 | 80 | 90 | 100 |

Percent

Buy Now, Pay Later

In some cases, borrowing money is both necessary and smart. For instance, taking out a loan to buy a house is usually a wise financial decision. But in other cases, borrowing money leads to overspending and going into debt. Knowing about credit cards, installment purchases, and bank loans will help you avoid these problems. It will also help make sure that you'll be able to borrow money if you ever need to.

Paying the Price

Jin couldn't believe it! In today's mail, she received two more offers from credit card companies. She hadn't kept count, but she knew she'd received at least 20 such offers over the past few months.

Jin had seen a program on TV about credit card companies offering cards to college students. These companies know that students often need money. And needing money makes some students eager to have credit cards. But using credit cards puts many college students into serious debt.

One of Jin's friends was in that situation. Connor had started using a credit card to pay his utility bills and other expenses. Soon, he had "maxed out" the card. That meant he had spent all he could using it.

Then, Connor got a second card and started taking out cash at ATMs. He even used some of that money to make payments on the first card. But using the card to get cash involved paying high service fees. Connor also paid high fees for making his payments late and even missing a few of them.

Connor was paying another price, too. The stress of dealing with all this was terrible! He got phone calls about his debts all day long.

Jin had one credit card. She used it for emergencies, like when she had to get her car fixed last winter. She also used it to treat herself from time to time. Over Thanksgiving, she'd used the card to buy a bus ticket to Denver, where she visited a friend.

But Jin kept up with payments on the card. In fact, she paid more each month than she had to. She didn't want to end up in Connor's situation.

CHAPTER 1

Dangers of Debt

Many people have some debt at some time in their lives. For instance, most people who own homes have borrowed the money and are paying it off over many years.

But piling up debt and staying in debt are ***troublesome***, for several reasons:

→ You're legally required to pay back the money you owe. No matter what happens in the future, part of your money will have to be spent paying for the debts you took on today.

Troublesome

Causing worry or upset.

[FACT]

Debt for the Average American

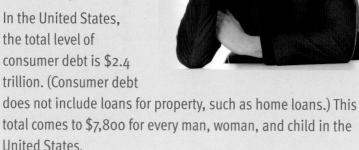

- 80% of Americans are in debt. On average, 12% of Americans' income goes to paying off loans (including home loans).

- In the United States, the total level of consumer debt is $2.4 trillion. (Consumer debt does not include loans for property, such as home loans.) This total comes to $7,800 for every man, woman, and child in the United States.

- 33% of Americans' debt is from revolving credit, which is mainly credit card debt. The other 67% is from debts such as vehicle loans or student loans.

- 66% of college students graduate with debt from student loans. The average amount owed is $23,186.

- Approximately 180 million Americans have credit cards. The average person has 9 credit cards, for a total of 1.5 billion credit cards in use.

- Among Americans with credit cards, the average amount owed on the cards is about $16,000.

- Each year, 2.0 to 2.5 million Americans get help from a credit counselor. Among these people, the average amount of debt is $43,000.

→ You must pay interest to borrow money. The higher the interest rate, the more it costs you to be in debt.

→ Debt costs time and energy too. You'll have extra records to keep, and you'll have to pay attention to when your payments are due. If you're late or miss a payment, you'll pay a service fee. And that adds even more to your debt.

→ Debt can pile up. When you're paying off a debt plus the interest, it's easy to run short of cash. You may have to borrow more money just to cover your basic needs.

Why Go into Debt?

Most debt can be avoided. Often, you can save the money needed to buy something and then pay cash for it. But some debts are *unavoidable*, especially in emergency situations. For instance, some people go into debt after having an illness or accident, because they have to pay high medical bills.

Unavoidable
Impossible to avoid.
Necessary.

Some debts are really ***investments***. For example, the money you spend on a college loan or a home loan will pay off in the future.

Investment

A purchase that's made to earn a profit or gain in value.

Good Reasons to Borrow Money

- **To buy a house:** The average home in the United States costs just over $200,000. Few people can afford to pay for a house all at once. So, having a *mortgage*, or home loan, is necessary for most Americans. Borrowing money allows paying for a house in monthly payments over up to 30 years.

- **To buy a car:** The average new car costs $28,400. Again, most people can't afford to pay cash for something so expensive. Americans usually borrow 80% of the money needed to buy a new car.

- **To go to college:** Getting a four-year degree can cost up to $25,000 a year, or $100,000 to $125,000 total. Because of this high cost, most students need to take out loans to pay for their education. To avoid taking out loans for college some students opt to go less expensive institutions that offer the education they want. Then they don't spend years paying off the loans they take out.

Your Credit Rating

When you get a loan or buy something on credit, your payment activities are reported to credit reporting agencies. These agencies are companies that collect information about your bill paying and borrowing history.

Then, the agencies provide that information to lenders, rental agencies, employers, and others. They look at the information to see if you are responsible with money. Your credit rating is like your financial "report card."

Having a poor credit rating may keep you from getting a loan, a place to live, and even a job. That's why it's so important to pay your bills on time and to not take on too much debt. Making regular payments on your debt also helps establish your good credit rating.

Building Your Credit Rating

If you've never borrowed money or bought anything on credit, you may have no credit rating at all. This makes you an unknown credit risk. Being in this situation can be troublesome too. It may result in your getting turned down for loans, rental housing, and so on.

If you're just getting started, think about the best way to establish your credit history. A local credit counseling service can often give you free or low-cost advice. Ask your public librarian to help you locate one.

[FACT]

Credit Reporting Agencies

The three main US credit reporting agencies are Equifax, Experian, and TransUnion. These companies operate according to the Fair Credit Reporting Act (FCRA). The FCRA requires each credit reporting agency to provide you with one free credit report a year. If you have been turned down for a loan or credit card, you can get a free report within 30 days. The bank or business that turned you down must tell you which agency provided negative credit information about you.

CHAPTER **2**

Using Credit Cards

Do you know what happens when you charge something on a credit card?

A machine at the store reads your card's account number and prints it on a slip of paper. The credit slip shows the name of the store, the date, and the total amount of your purchase.

After you make sure the total is correct, you sign the slip. Once you've signed, the credit company pays the store and sends you the bill later.

Always keep copies of your signed credit slips. You may need them to prove you've been overcharged or billed incorrectly.

Benefits of Using Credit Cards

Using a credit card can be very convenient:

→ You can purchase something right away and pay for it later.

→ You can purchase things over the phone or the Internet.

→ You have a **reliable** way to pay for unexpected situations, such as emergencies.

→ Your monthly bill serves as a record of your purchases.

Risks of Using Credit Cards

Sometimes, having a credit card makes shopping a little too easy. You might run into these problems:

→ If you're not careful, you'll spend much more than you can afford.

→ If you can't afford to pay the whole balance each month, you'll carry the unpaid amount as a debt.

Reliable
Dependable and trustworthy.

→ A credit card debt is one of the costliest debts you can have. The interest on the unpaid balance can be up to 40% a year! That's much higher than the interest banks charge for most types of loans.

→ If you can't pay the whole bill when it's due, you must make at least a small minimum payment. Otherwise, you'll be charged a fee called a *late charge*. Late charges can add a lot to your debt.

→ If you pay late or skip payments, your credit rating will be damaged.

[FACT]

The Costs of Using Credit Cards

- **Interest:** When you don't pay off what you owe on a credit card each month, you're charged interest on the amount you owe. Interest rates on credit cards range from 0% up to 40%. Usually, the interest rate goes up the longer you have an unpaid balance.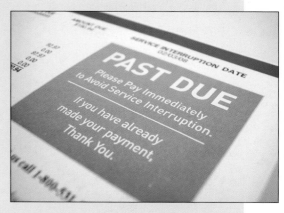

- **Late fees and fees for missed payments:** When you use a credit card, you're usually given 30 days to pay the amount owed or to make a minimum payment. If you pay late or don't make the payment at all, you'll be charged a fee of around $30.

- **Annual fees:** Some credit cards charge annual fees of as much as $75 or $100.

Shopping for the Best Deal

If you decide to apply for a credit card, shop around first. Most banks and some businesses offer credit cards.

Some credit cards are much less expensive than others. Ask these questions before accepting any credit card:

→ Is there an annual fee for service? If so, how much?

→ What is the **APR (Annual Percentage Rate)**? The higher the APR, the more it will cost to pay off a credit card debt.

→ What is the payment "grace period"? Look for a **grace period** of at least 24 days. That will give you more than three weeks to pay the full balance without being charged interest.

APR (Annual Percentage Rate)

What you pay to borrow money each year for the entire term of the loan. It includes the annual interest rate plus any other fees.

Grace period

The time after a payment due date that a lender will accept a late payment without charging a penalty.

Tips for Smart and Safe Credit Card Use

- Pay off the amount owed each month. If you make only the minimum payment and carry a balance, you'll likely increase your level of debt over time.

- Research before you accept a credit card. Before you sign up for a credit card, read the terms and rates. Make sure you know exactly what you're getting into. Look for cards with low interest rates and no or low fees.

- Have only a few cards. The fewer cards you have, the better. Having more credit cards means having to keep track of more accounts. Having a lot of cards also increases the risk of identity theft.

- Pay your bills on time. Paying on time will help you avoid late fees and interest payments. Making timely payments will also improve your credit rating.

Credit Card Use by Young Adults

Young adults often use credit cards to buy things they can't afford and put off the payments. In a way, having a credit card is like having a short-term loan. For many young adults, though, paying off that loan isn't always easy.

Consider these facts about credit card use among young adults:

- Most people under age 35 got their first credit card when they were 21.

- 41% of young adults (ages 18 to 29) usually pay only the minimum per month.

- Since 1989, credit card debt for the average young person has increased by 47%.

- College undergraduates have an average credit card debt of $3,173.

CHAPTER 3

Borrowing Money

Always save as much money as you can before buying an expensive item, like a car. And if you still need a loan, try to make the biggest *down payment* possible.

The larger the down payment, the less money you'll have to borrow. And the smaller the *principal*, the fewer the payments you'll have to make and the less you'll pay in interest.

Down payment

How much of your own money you put toward the cost of something at the time of purchase.

Principal

The amount of money you borrow.

Shopping for a Loan

Banks, finance companies, and credit unions all lend money. In addition, car dealers and other businesses often *finance* large purchases, such as cars. Shop around before

Finance
To provide the funding for.

you accept a loan from a car dealer. You can usually find a less expensive loan through a bank or credit union.

First, decide how much you need to borrow. Then ask the lender these questions:

→ How many monthly payments will I have to make?

→ What is the interest rate or finance charge?

→ How much will each monthly payment be?

→ Is there a fine for paying off the loan early?

Sources of Car Loans

- **Banks:** If you have a checking account or credit card account with a bank, that's a good place to get a car loan. But check interest rates at several banks before you agree to a loan.

- **Credit unions:** Credit unions often have lower interest rates than banks. You can sometimes join a credit union through your employer or profession.

- **Finance companies:** Finance companies usually charge higher interest rates than banks. But a finance company may be more willing to give you a loan if you have a low credit rating.

- **Dealer financing:** Some car dealers offer loans, but the interest rates are often high. Customers with excellent credit may get a low interest rate, however.

Applying for a Loan

To get a loan, you must fill out an application. It will ask for information about where you work, how much money you make, and what debts you have.

What you write on the application is important. Why? The lender will use this information to decide if you're a good credit risk.

Co-signer

Someone who agrees to share responsibility for another person's loan.

If you have poor credit or no credit history, you may be asked to get a *co-signer*. That

person must have a good credit rating. He or she must also agree to pay off the loan, if you don't. He or she will need to fill out a loan application too.

Stating Your Income

When you fill out the loan application, be sure to include all of your income, not just your earnings from your job. For example, if you receive payments for disability or Social Security, that money counts as income. And if you earn money on investments or savings, that's income too.

Getting Pre-Approved

Getting pre-approved for a car loan lets you shop as if you have cash. In most cases, when you find the car you want, you can drive it away. If you get pre-approved, you'll know exactly how much you can spend and what your payments will be. You might also be able to work out a lower price for the car.

To get pre-approved, fill out a loan application. You may be able to do this in person, over the telephone, or online. The approval process may take up to several days, but it will be time well spent. Buying a car will be a lot simpler if you've been pre-approved.

CHAPTER 4

Installment Purchases

What if you don't have a credit card or a loan and want to buy something expensive, like a piece of furniture or a new TV? Making a purchase with an ***installment*** plan is another way to buy on credit.

Installment

One in a series of payments made to buy an item or pay off a debt.

Usually, you begin by making a small down payment. That's your first installment. Then, you pay weekly or monthly installments until you've paid the debt in full.

Remember that you're borrowing money when you make installment purchases. That means you're paying interest. Installment plans usually charge higher interest rates than any other forms of loans.

Consumer Protection Agencies

Many people are unhappy with installment plans after agreeing to them. That's why many of the complaints made to consumer protection agencies are about installment purchases.

Every state has a consumer protection agency or office of consumer affairs. So does the US government. These agencies perform the following functions:

- Enforce laws that protect consumers
- Provide licenses for doing certain jobs
- Tell consumers about their rights
- Help consumers avoid unfair practices
- Help settle consumer complaints about poor work or service

Layaway Plans

One kind of installment plan is called *layaway*. With a layaway plan, the store sets aside your purchase until you've paid for it in full.

Buying on layaway is convenient for many people. For example, some people buy Christmas gifts using layaway. They select the gifts months in advance. That way, they're able to pay them off by the holidays.

But there are some risks to this type of purchasing plan:

→ What if the store goes out of business before you finish paying for your purchase? You could lose all your payments and not ever get the item.

→ What are the charges for using layaway? Layaway plans often include a lot of hidden charges. So before you agree to such a plan, be sure to ask for a written agreement. Be clear about exactly how often and how much you must pay.

→ What if you miss a payment? If you miss a payment or don't pay off the item on time, the store might sell it and keep the money you've already paid. Protect yourself! Make sure the agreement states that the store will refund your money if it sells your item. Get it in writing.

[FACT]

Online Layaway

When the US economy went bad around 2007–2008, several online layaway companies started up. People started using them to buy items without running up credit card debt. Using online layaway also helps people budget for items they really want.

Here's how two of these online companies operate:

- eLayaway lets the shopper decide how many payments to make and for what amount. The company debits the shopper's bank account, taking out each payment at a scheduled time. After the item's been paid off, it's shipped within a few days. eLayaway charges interest on each transaction of 1.9% to 3%.

- Lay-Away.com has the shopper pay by check or money order. The company gets paid a percentage of the cost of the item by the store. The shopper doesn't pay a service fee. Again, once the item has been paid off, it's sent to the shopper.

Rent-to-Own Plans

With a *rent-to-own plan*, you get to take home the item before you pay it off. Then, you make weekly or monthly payments—much like paying rent. Some people buy furniture, appliances, computers, and electronics with rent-to-own plans.

Most rent-to-own plans have what's called a *90-days-same-as-cash option*. Paying off the item in 90 days will save you from paying high interest and service fees. If you can't pay off the item that quickly, then choose a plan that fits your budget. Just remember that the longer you pay on the item, the more it will end up costing.

With some rent-to-own plans, the item is yours when the rental period is over. But other plans end with what's called a ***"balloon" payment***. If you can't make that final payment, you must return the item. And you won't get a refund of the money you've already paid.

Like layaway plans, rent-to-own plans have some risks:

→ What if the item is stolen or damaged? You'll still have to pay for it. Protect yourself by getting

"Balloon" payment	Repossess
A large payment due at the end of an installment plan or loan.	To take back a purchased item because of nonpayment.

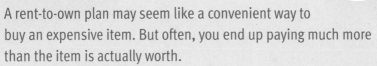

a liability waiver. It's a kind of insurance that protects you against loss or damage. It will cost extra money, but it's probably worth it.

→ What if you fall behind on your payments? The store can **repossess** the item. And in most cases, the store won't refund the money you've already paid.

In tough economic times, rent-to-own plans offer a way for many Americans to buy expensive items. In fact, renting-to-own might be the only way some people can buy these items. Even people with bad credit or no credit usually get approved for these installment plans. In most cases, no credit check is required.

You Do the Math!

A rent-to-own plan may seem like a convenient way to buy an expensive item. But often, you end up paying much more than the item is actually worth.

Suppose you decide to buy a digital camera that costs $565. You make a down payment of $15, and you get to take home the camera. You're excited about getting to use it right away!

The rent-to-own plan says that you have to pay $6.22 a week for five years. But multiply $6.22 a week by 260 weeks (five years). Then add your $15 down payment to that. In the end, you'll pay $1,622.40 for a $565 camera.

That's almost triple the original price! The interest alone will cost you $1,067.40. That's a lot of wasted money.

Improving Your Budgeting Skills

You probably know about how much you spend a month on rent, utilities, transportation, food, and clothing. Or do you? Many people are surprised when they keep track of exactly where and why they spend their money. Tracking your expenses and having a budget will help you manage your money wisely.

Where Does the Money Go?

Jamie's friends were talking about going to Mexico for a winter vacation. She really wanted to go, but she wasn't sure she could afford it. It's not that the trip would be expensive. Her friends had found a travel package with a low price. The problem was that Jamie never seemed to have any money.

"Why is that?" she wondered.

To answer that question, Jamie started keeping track of her expenses. She carried a small notebook with her and wrote down everything she bought all day. Then every night, she looked over the day's notes. She added up exactly how much money she'd spent. She also looked carefully at what she'd spent the money on.

After only a week, Jamie understood why she never had any money! She was spending a lot on small, unnecessary things. For instance, every day, she bought two cups of coffee at the café next to the office

where she worked. At $5 a cup, that was $10 a day, $50 a week, and $200 a month. Cutting back to one cup a day would save $100 a month!

Another expense that caught Jamie's attention was eating out. She bought a salad or a sandwich at the office cafeteria every day. And two or three times a week, she ate out with friends. Jamie figured out that she averaged $20 a day eating out. That came to about $600 a month!

Tracking her expenses made Jamie realize she'd developed some expensive habits. Cutting back on several things would save her hundreds of dollars a month. That money would pay for a winter vacation and much, much more.

CHAPTER **1**

Your Goal:
A Balanced Budget

The Basics of Budgeting

Probably the best way to
manage your money is to have a
budget. A budget has two main
parts: *income* and *expenses*.

Your goal in creating
a budget is to make your
expenses equal your income.

Budget

A plan for earning and spending money during a certain time period.

Income

Money that's earned or received.

Expense

Something that's purchased.

When they do, you have a *balanced* budget. You are earning and spending the same amount of money.

What if you spend *less* than you earn? That's good! To make your budget balance, you could add "savings" as an expense. You'll "spend" this extra money by putting it into a savings account.

Technological Budgeting Tools

A number of computer programs and Web sites provide budgeting tools. Get help creating a budget and tracking your expenses using any of the following:

AceMoney	Buxfer	Quicken
BudgetPulse	Mint	YNAB (You Need a Budget)
BudgetTracker	Mvelopes	

Some of these tools also perform these functions:

- Track different kinds of expenses, such as groceries and transportation.
- Link to bank accounts to automatically record when money is deposited and withdrawn.
- Write checks and pay bills online.
- Split bills that are shared by several people, such as roommates.
- Create pie charts and graphs of financial information, such as expenses.

What if you spend *more* than you earn? That's bad! To make your budget balance, you could find a way to reduce your expenses. You might have to go without something or cut back in some area. To balance your budget, you could also find a way to increase your income. You might get a part-time job, for instance.

Why Have a Budget?

Budgeting forces you to plan ahead. It also makes you identify what you spend and what you earn. Writing down your income and expenses makes you more aware of them.

By balancing your budget, you'll be better able to manage your money. Specifically, you'll be better able to control your spending, handle unexpected expenses, stay out of debt, and find ways to save.

A Sample Monthly Budget

A budget can cover a year, a month, or even a week. But most people budget on a monthly basis.

See the basic monthly budget on the next page.

You can see that this budget is balanced. The "Total Expenses" listed at the bottom equals the "Total Income" listed near the top.

Monthly Budget

Income

Job at Tech World	$600.00
Job at Larson's Landscapes	$240.00
Total Income	$840.00

Expenses

Fixed Expenses

Room and board	$400.00
Internet fee (my share)	$21.00
Cable TV (my share)	$15.00
Phone (my share)	$14.50

Variable Expenses

Laundry ($5/week x 4 weeks)	$20.00
Bus fare	$31.50
Clothing	$25.00
Personal care/drugstore	$15.00
Haircut	$18.00
School supplies	$20.00
Snack food ($10/week x 4 weeks)	$40.00
Entertainment ($25/week x 4 weeks)	$100.00

Savings

College fund	$100.00
Gifts/Holiday fund	$20.00

Total Expenses	$840.00

Kinds of Expenses

Notice in the sample budget that two kinds of expenses are shown: *fixed expenses* and *variable expenses*. What's the difference between them?

→ Fixed expenses always stay the same. They include most living expenses, such as room and board and monthly utilities. In many cases, these are expenses you've agreed to pay. For budgeting, you can't change a fixed expense to make your budget balance.

→ Variable expenses can change, for several reasons. You might need to spend more or less on something during one month versus another—clothes, for instance. Or you might choose to spend more or less on something—perhaps entertainment. For budgeting, you can use variable expenses to make your budget balance.

Cutting Back on Entertainment

If you're spending more money than you're taking in, think about cutting back on entertainment. Review these common entertainment expenses:

- Eating out
- Going to movies
- Internet fees
- Cable or satellite TV fees
- Movie rentals

- Hobbies
- Weekend activities
- Tickets to events
- Travel
- Athletic memberships

[FACT]

Budget Recommendations for Young Adults

Are you having trouble setting up a budget? Think about dividing your income into these types and ranges of expenses:

① Housing: 25% to 35%

② Utilities: 4% to 7%

③ Food (both groceries and restaurants): 10% to 15%

④ Transportation (includes car expenses, if you own a car): 5% to 15%

⑤ Personal care (includes clothing): 5% to 10%

⑥ Health care (monthly insurance rate plus out-of-pocket expenses): 10% to 15%

⑦ Loan paybacks (not including car payments): 7% to 15%

⑧ Entertainment: 1% to 5%

CHAPTER 2

Keeping a Personal Expense Record

Before you can budget your money, you must gather certain facts. You need to know the following:

→ Your monthly income, including earnings from work and other sources

→ Your monthly fixed expenses

→ Your monthly variable expenses

→ Your monthly savings

In addition, take a look at your expenses and identify any that are *excessive*. Think about what you could easily cross off your budget to save money.

Excessive

Too much. More than is acceptable or allowed.

Organizing Your Expenses

To get a clear picture of your spending, start keeping a personal expense record. Be sure to list everything you earn and spend every week.

Jodie decided to keep a personal expense record. She used a small notebook to list her expenses and hold her receipts. At the end of each week, she checked the receipts against her notebook to make sure she'd recorded everything. Then, she organized her expenses under budget *categories*.

Categories

Types or classes.

Tips for Keeping a Daily Expense Log

- Record every penny you spend throughout the day. Don't forget debit card uses and ATM withdrawals.

- Use cash as much as possible. Paying for something with "real money" will make you more likely to write it down.

- Note each expense and what it was for. Keep receipts and make notes on them.

- Set up your log with categories of expenses. Record different types of expenses in individual columns or on separate pages.

- Use your daily log to determine your average weekly expenses. And use that information to create a monthly budget.

Here are some of the expenses Jodie recorded:

JUNE 12

Entertainment
Gym:	$10.50
DVD rental:	$6.50
RapDap concert:	$45.75
RapDap CD:	$18.50

Personal Care
Toothbrush:	$2.59

Food
Turkey sandwich:	$5.40
Bananas:	$1.09

Transportation
Light-rail pass:	$10.00
Bus pass:	$4.50

Other
Birthday gift:	$12.00

Monthly Totals

After tracking her spending for a month, Jodie made this expense chart:

Category	Week 1	Week 2	Week 3	Week 4	Total
Room/Board	$300.00	—	—	—	$300.00
School lunch	$6.49	$22.50	$14.50	$10.98	$54.47
Phone	$15.20	—	—	—	$15.20
Transportation	$14.50	$14.50	$14.50	$14.50	$58.00
Personal care	$2.59	$15.40	$3.25	$4.92	$26.16
Clothing	$99.40	$22.38	$14.98	—	$136.76
Entertainment	$81.25	$17.00	$52.00	$36.99	$187.24
Other	$6.60	—	$3.75	$9.65	$20.00
Total Monthly Expenses					$797.83

Notice how Jodie used the categories she'd set up to organize different types of expenses. Then, she figured out the weekly amount for each category. The weekly totals gave her the information she needed to create a monthly budget.

Excessive Spending

Jodie's income is $800 a month, and she has trouble saving. This month, she spent all but $2.17 of her earnings. She needs to identify her excessive spending to find places to cut back.

[FACT]

Top Money Wasters

Each of the following money wasters can cost you hundreds of dollars a year! Where can you cut back?

1. ATM fees
2. Lottery tickets
3. Gourmet coffee
4. Cigarettes
5. Infomercial buys (such as Snuggies and Magic Bullet blender)
6. Brand-name groceries (instead of store-brand foods)
7. Eating out
8. Unused gym memberships

Jody studied her three biggest monthly expenses. Her biggest expense—room and board—is a fixed expense. She can't change that. Next, she looked at her clothing and entertainment expenses. She's spending too much on both these items.

[FACT]

Free Online Courses in Money Management

- Take Control of Your Money (Extension and Outreach at Iowa State University): www.extension.iastate .edu/finances/personal/ take_control_course.htm

- Fundamentals of Financial Planning (OpenCourseWare at University of California, Irvine): http://ocw.uci.edu/courses/course .aspx?id=12

- Money 101: A Step-by-Step Guide to Gaining Control of Your Financial Life (CNN Money Magazine): http://money.cnn.com/ magazines/moneymag/money101/

- Invest in Yourself (American Financial Solutions, IRIS Education at Seattle Community Colleges Television): www.iriseducation .org/afs/

- Balance Track money management course: www.balancetrack .org/moneymanagement/index.html

- Investing for Your Future (Extension, University of Minnesota): www.extension.org/pages/10984/investing-for-your-future

Next month, Jodie will budget $100 for clothing and $100 for entertainment. If she sticks to her plan, she will save $124. That will give her money to put into savings.

Smart Phone "Apps"

Dozens of smart phone applications, or "apps," are available for budgeting and tracking expenses. Many of them are available for free. For instance, some banks provide free apps to their customers. Other apps are free only during a trial period, but then involve a cost. Read the user agreement carefully to find out if you'll be charged after a certain time.

Some budgeting programs and Web sites also have smart phone versions. Both Mint and YNAB (You Need a Budget) are available as apps.

Check with your mobile carrier to find out what apps are available for your phone.

CHAPTER **3**

Typical Budget Adjustments

When you create your first budget, you'll probably forget a few things. Most people do!

After you add these things to your budget, you'll have to balance it again. It's fairly simple to make *typical adjustments* and rebalance your budget.

Typical
Usual or normal.

Adjustment
A small change or correction.

Adjusting Jack's Monthly Budget

Jack certainly forgot a few things in creating his monthly budget.
He forgot that he'd need an extra $35 for a new textbook this month.
He also forgot that he needed $18 to fix his bike.

Jack added these two extra variable expenses to his budget. You can
see where he's written them in on the following page.

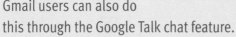

Reducing Cell Phone Costs

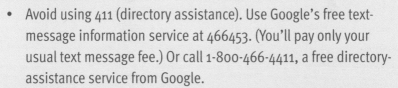

- Switch plans. Get a plan with fewer minutes.

- Text for free. Some phone apps use your e-mail account to send and receive messages. Gmail users can also do this through the Google Talk chat feature.

- Avoid using 411 (directory assistance). Use Google's free text-message information service at 466453. (You'll pay only your usual text message fee.) Or call 1-800-466-4411, a free directory-assistance service from Google.

- Use Voice-over Internet protocol (VoIP). If you no longer have a landline, use a VoIP service, such as Skype or Vonage. It allows you to make and receive calls over the Internet at a huge savings.

- Ask for discounts. Talk to your cell phone service provider about discounts or reduced fees. They're sometimes available if you ask for them.

Monthly Budget

Income
    Job at Tech World $600.00
    Job at Larson's Landscapes $240.00
Total Income $840.00

Expenses
Fixed Expenses
    Room and board $400.00
    Internet fee (my share) $21.00
    Cable TV (my share) $15.00
    Phone (my share) $14.50
Variable Expenses
    Laundry ($5/week x 4 weeks) $20.00
    Bus fare $31.50
    Clothing $25.00
    Personal care/drugstore $15.00
    Haircut $18.00
    School supplies $20.00
    Snack food ($10/week x 4 weeks) $40.00
    Entertainment ($25/week x 4 weeks) $100.00
    Books $35.00
    Repairs $18.00

Savings
    College fund $100.00
    Gifts/Holiday fund $20.00

Total Expenses   ~~$840.00~~
                            $893.00

Reducing Transportation Costs

- **Rethink a car purchase**. Buying a car involves paying more than the purchase price. Before you buy, think about the costs of insurance, registration, gas, repairs, and maintenance.

- **Buy a car you can pay cash for**. Don't go into debt to buy a car. Buy a vehicle you can purchase without taking out a loan.

- **Sell or park your car**. If you can't keep up with the costs of operating your car, then don't drive it. Either sell it or park it.

- **Make regular maintenance checks**. In the long run, keeping up with maintenance lowers the cost of repairs.

- **Join a carpool or take a bus or train**. Sharing a ride or using public transportation is cheaper than driving your own car.

- **Look for cheaper parking**. If you have to pay to park, look for the cheapest lot or ramp available. This might mean having further to walk and thus needing extra time.

- **Ride a bike or walk**. These are the cheapest options of all. Try to live close to work or school, so you don't need to own a car or pay for public transportation.

Adjusting Expenses

Now, Jack's budget doesn't balance. His expenses are $53 more than his income. How can he keep his budget balanced when extra expenses come up?

Jack can take money away from other expense items. Then, he can use that money to cover the new expenses. Remember that he can't change fixed expenses. But he can take money from variable expenses or from savings.

Saving Money Eating at Home

- Don't eat out.
- Buy store-brand products, not brand-name products.
- Grow your own tomatoes and other foods.
- Use the grocery coupons provided in newspapers and online.
- Don't buy ready-made foods. Cook foods from scratch, making them all on your own.
- Shop at a warehouse or low-cost food store once a month to stock up.
- Plan meals around items on sale at the grocery store.
- Plan meals two weeks ahead, and buy only what you need to fix them.
- Keep a grocery list on your refrigerator. Add items as you run out of them.
- Avoid buying things on impulse.

Jack refuses to take money from his savings. "There must be another way," he thinks to himself. So, that leaves variable expenses as the place to make adjustments.

Jack decides to cut entertainment by $40 and clothing by $13. Making these changes will cover the extra $53 in expenses. And by adjusting his budget, he now has a clear picture of what he must do to avoid spending more than he earns.

Saving Money Eating at Restaurants

- Look for coupons in your mailbox, in newspapers, and online.
- Go out for breakfast or lunch, not dinner. (Dinner costs more.)
- Snack before eating out to reduce your appetite.
- Order a small item, or split something with a friend.
- Drink tapwater. Beverages are expensive, especially alcohol.

- If you drink alcohol, have a drink at home before you go out.
- If you drink wine, order the house wine, which is usually cheaper.
- Ethnic restaurants often offer more food for the money.
- Take advantage of all-you-can-eat buffets.
- Ask about menu specials. They are often less expensive than other items.
- Check for dollar menus at fast-food restaurants.
- Skip dessert, or split one.

CHAPTER 4

Handling Unexpected Expenses

Julie's very good about following her budget. She's also good about saving. She has $1,018 in her savings account.

But then it happened: Julie got a toothache. After a trip to the dentist, she now owes $650.

Next, Julie's computer broke down. It's about a year old, so it's not under *warranty* anymore. Making the repairs will cost $249.

All of a sudden, Julie has $899 in unexpected expenses! She has enough money in savings to cover these expenses. But she doesn't like to use her savings unless she has no other choice.

Warranty

A written promise or contract about a product's quality. A warranty usually offers to repair or replace a product that doesn't work.

Julie found out that she can pay her dentist's bill in monthly installments. And she's decided to use her credit card to pay for the computer repairs.

Julie's Payment Plan

Julie's figured out how to adjust her monthly budget to pay her new debts. Here's her payment plan:

New Expense	Payment Plan	Budget Adjustments
$650 doctor bill	Pay $56.87/month for 12 months Interest paid: $32.44 Total paid: $682.44	Add: $56.87 monthly payment as fixed expense Subtract: $50 from monthly payment into college/emergency savings Subtract: $6.87 from monthly payment into gift/holiday fund
$249 computer repair	Pay using credit card Pay $25/month for 12 months Interest paid: about $50 Total paid: $299	Add: $25 monthly payment as fixed expense Subtract: $25 a month from entertainment expenses

[FACT]

Reducing Dental Bills

One way to lower your dental bills is to ask the dentist for a discount. According to a national survey, 64% of the people who asked for a discount received one. Yet only 10% of the people said they'd ever asked!

Don't be afraid to talk to your dentist about a discount. When you do, be honest and direct. Say that having good dental care is important to you. But explain that you can't afford to pay large bills.

If the dentist agrees, he or she will usually offer a discount of 30% to 50%. And if you accept the reduced amount, you'll be expected to pay it with cash right away.

A Better Payment Plan

Julie isn't satisfied with this plan, for several reasons. She'll have to cut back on entertainment expenses for a year to pay off the credit card bill. Also, she'll be saving much less every month. And worst of all, this plan will cost her more than $80 in interest!

Julie decided to talk to the manager of her bank. He suggested taking out a savings account loan. This low-cost way to borrow money will charge only 8.1% interest. Julie can move $1,000 from her savings account to a two-year certificate of deposit (CD). The bank will accept Julie's CD as **collateral** for the new loan.

Extended Warranties

When you buy a new appliance or electronic item, it's covered by the manufacturer's warranty. That warranty is probably good for 90 days. If you want a longer period, you can buy an *extended warranty*.

The extended warranty will be provided by the store you're buying the appliance from. It will probably cost around $100 and be good for two or three years. During that time, the warranty will likely cover the cost of parts and labor for making repairs. It may also cover maintenance checks and normal wear-and-tear.

It makes sense to buy an extended warranty for an expensive product that's difficult to fix, such as a computer. But you probably don't need to buy an extended warranty for an inexpensive product, such as a microwave. It could be a waste of money. If you've shopped well and bought a good-quality product, you shouldn't need to repair it for many years to come.

Collateral

An item that's provided to guarantee a loan will be paid back. If the person with the loan doesn't repay it, the lender gets to keep the item provided as collateral. For example, for an automobile loan, the vehicle is the collateral.

Building an Emergency Fund

Financial advisors recommend having an emergency fund. You should save enough money to cover at least three to six months' worth of expenses.

How can you build your emergency fund?

1. **Start small.** Saving $10 a week is better than nothing. Look at your budget to figure out where you can cut expenses. Then over time, gradually increase the amount you save.

2. **Set a goal.** If three months' expenses sounds like too much, try saving $1,000. When you reach that goal, increase it.

3. **Open an account.** Keep your emergency savings separate from your regular savings and checking accounts. Also make regular deposits. And then, save this money for use only in major emergencies.

Julie will have two years to pay off the loan, and she can make monthly payments. If she doesn't, the bank will take what she still owes from her savings account. The faster Julie pays off the loan, the less interest she'll be charged.

The CD will earn 3.9% interest. This will help make up for the interest Julie's paying, leaving her with 4.2% yearly interest. In all, she'll pay less than half as much in interest compared to her original plan.

Julie took out a $900 savings account loan and paid the dentist and computer repair bills in full. She added to her budget a $78 fixed monthly expense to repay her loan in one year. She reduced some variable expenses. But she was still able to put money into savings each month.

Tips for Making Your Budget Work

1. **Be positive.** Don't focus on what you're giving up by budgeting. Instead, think about the goals you're trying to achieve.

2. **Be committed.** Try to keep your budget goals in mind. If you're losing sight of them, push yourself. For instance, try to save a little more or pay off a debt a little sooner. Also be sure to reward yourself for reaching each goal.

3. **Be realistic.** Start with small goals you can achieve in short amounts of time. As you reach those goals, set bigger goals with longer time frames.

Word List

access	charges	depressed	expensive
accident	charity	desire	experiencing
according	cheap	detailed	extended
accurate	checkbook	determine	
achieve	checklist	develop	fee
activities	chemical	device	financial
adjustment	collateral	disability	fine
advertising	college	discount	fixed
advisor	column	distant	frugal
agency	commercial	dividends	function
agreement	committed	dividing	fund
annual	complaint	document	
appliance	compulsive	donate	genius
application	consequences		guarantee
approve	consumer	eager	guidelines
ATM	contain	earnings	
attract	contribution	economic	hardship
automatic	convenient	eliminate	household
available	convince	emergency	
	co-signer	employee	identify
balance	counselor	employer	ignore
bargain	credit	encourage	impulse
behavior	creditor	enforce	income
branch	customer	entertainment	influence
budget		entry	information
bulk	damage	error	installment
	debit	eventually	interest
cancelled	debt	excessive	investment
careless	degree	exchange	involve
carpool	delay	excite	item
categories	deposit	expectations	

Word List

lender
license
loan
log

maintenance
manage
manager
marketing
medical
membership
minimum

negative

online
option
organization
organize
overdrawn
overspending

participate
password
penalty
perform
personalized
polite
practices
pre-approve
pressure

principal
priorities
process
product
professional
profit
program
promise
protect

quality
quantity

rating
realistic
receipt
recommendation
reconcile
records
recreation
recurring
refund
register
release
reliable
rely
repair
replace
repossess
request
research

resist
responsibility
responsible
retirement
review
reward
risk

savings
scam
scheduled
scheme
security
series
serious
shift
shipped
signature
situation
software
solution
source
statement
storage
stress
substitute
survey

technological
temptation
tense

threatening
thrifty
track
transaction
transfer
transportation
treatment
trial
tuition
typical

unavoidable
unit
unknown
unsatisfactory
urge
utilities

values
variable
vehicle
verify

warranty
withdrawal

Index

Applications ("Apps"), for budgets/budgeting, 103
Automated Teller Machines (ATMs), 39, 40–41, 101
Automatic transactions
deposits, 55
payments, 42, 45, 47, 52, 53

Balancing,
of checking account, 23, 44, 45, 50, 52. *See also* Reconciling
Bank records, 22–25. *See also specific types*
Bank statements
example of, 51
online availability of, 53
purposes of, 25, 42, 48. *See also* Reconciling
Banks/Banking, 36–41
choosing of, 38–39
fees of, 39, 41, 46, 47, 53, 57
loans by. *See* Loans
mistakes in, 30
online forms of. *See* Online banking
reasons for using, 36–37
security of, 37, 40–41
services of, 39, 41, 53
types of, 38–39.
See also Checking accounts; Savings accounts

"Bounced checks," 46. *See also* Overdrawn
Budgets/Budgeting, 92–97, 99–103, 104–109
adjusting of, 93–94, 104–109
balancing of, 92–94
elements of, 92–94
examples of, 19, 94–95, 105–109
guidelines for, 97, 115
preparing for, 99–103
reasons for, 21, 94

Car loans/costs, 67, 77, 78, 81, 107
Cell phones, costs of, 105
Certificates of deposit (CDs), 57, 58, 112, 115
Check registers
electronic forms of, 52
example of, 51
purposes of, 23, 44
transactions recorded in, 23, 44–45, 48, 49–50
use in reconciling account, 49–52
Checking accounts, 42–47
bank statements for, 48–53
being overdrawn on, 46–47, 49, 53
checks written from. *See* Checks
fees of, 39, 41, 46, 47
interest paid on, 45

payments made from, 42, 45, 47, 50, 52
purposes of, 39, 42
reconciling of, 49–52
registers for. *See* Check registers
services with, 42, 47
transactions of, 42, 44–45, 48, 49–50
Checks
information printed on, 44
payment of, 46, 50
recording of, 23, 44–45, 48, 49–50. *See also* Check registers
writing of, 39, 43–44, 46–47
Computer programs/software, 52, 83, 103
Credit cards, 70–75
applying for, 73, 74
benefits of, 71
fees of, 66, 72, 73, 74
vs. debit cards, 43
debt from, 65, 71–72, 75
guidelines for, 74
interest charged on, 72, 73
payments on, 30, 31, 72, 74, 75
popularity of, 65, 75
risks of, 71–72
Credit rating, 68, 69, 72, 74
Credit unions, 38, 77, 78
Creditors, 30, 31

Debit cards, 42, 43, 45
Debt, 64–69
 average level of, 65
 from credit card use, 65,
  71–72, 75. *See also*
  Credit cards
 drawbacks of, 64–66
 loans to pay, 112–115
 reasons for, 64–65
Dental bills, 112
Deposit slips, 22. *See also*
  Deposits
Deposits
 automatic forms of, 55
 to checking accounts,
  42, 45
 records/recording of, 22,
  42, 45
 to savings accounts, 55

Emergency funds, 114. *See
  also* Saving money
Emergency situations, 66.
  See also Unexpected
  expenses
Expense reports/records,
  98–103
 as financial records, 21
 guidelines for, 99
 information for, 98–101
 purposes of, 99
Expenses
 basic kinds of, 13
 in budget, 92, 96
 priorities for, 15

recording/tracking of,
  21, 99–101. *See also*
  Expense reports/
  records
 reducing of, 101–103
 types of, 96. *See also*
  Needs vs. wants

Finance companies, 77, 78
Financial mistakes, 26–31
 in banking, 30
 in payments, 30
 in shopping, 27–28, 29
 and spending habits, 26
Financial records, 20–25
 online availability of, 52
 organizing of, 24
 privacy/security of, 24,
  25
 storage of, 25
 types of, 21–25. *See also
  specific types*

Great Depression, 37, 40
Groceries, cost of, 108

Home loans, 64, 65, 67

Identity theft, 74. *See also*
  Personal information
Income, 81, 92
Installment purchases,
  82–87
 complaints about, 83
 fees of, 83, 84, 86, 87
 interest charged on, 83,
  86, 87

payments on, 83, 84,
  86, 87
 process of, 83
 risks of, 84, 86–87
 types of, 84–87
Interest, rates/types of, 56,
  57, 58, 73

Layaway plans, 84, 85.
  See also Installment
  purchases
Living expenses, 13. *See
  also* Expenses
Loans, 76–81
 applying for, 68, 79–80,
  81
 for debt payments,
  112–115
 elements of, 76
 reasons for, 64, 65, 67,
  77, 81
 sources of, 77, 78

Money management
  courses, 102

Needs vs. wants, 14–19
 budgeting for, 19
 identification of, 16–19
"Nonsufficient funds," 46.
  See also Overdrawn

Online banking
 for bill paying, 24, 42,
  45, 47
 fees of, 53
 guidelines for, 53

scams in, 41
services with, 53
Online layaway, 85. *See
   also* Layaway plans
Overdrawn, in checking
   accounts, 46–47, 49,
   53. *See also* Checking
   accounts

Peer pressure, 9, 10, 12
Personal information,
   protection of, 41, 53.
   See also Identity theft
Pre-approval, for car loans,
   81. *See also* Car
   loans/costs

Receipts, 22
Reconciling, of checking
   accounts, 49–52
   bank records for, 48–49
   computer software for,
   52
   example of, 51–52
   process of, 49–50
Records. *See* Financial
   records
Registers, 23. *See also*
   Check registers
Rent-to-own plans, 86–87.
   See also Installment
   purchases
Restaurants, costs of
   eating at, 109
Returned checks, 46–47.
   See also Overdrawn

Saving money. *See also*
   Savings accounts
   budgeting for, 19, 55, 76,
   101–103
   for emergency fund, 114
   guidelines for, 55
   long-term benefits of,
   55, 56
   trends in, 59
Savings accounts, 54–59
   fees of, 39, 41, 57
   interest paid on, 56, 57
   loans tied to, 112–115
   and overdraft protection,
   47
   purposes of, 19, 54
   types of, 57
Scams, in banking, 40–41
Service charges, 23. *See
   also* subentry fees
   of under types of
   accounts/transactions
Shopping
   checklist for, 16
   as compulsion, 29
   mistakes in, 27–28, 29
   pleasure of, 17
Spending habits, 8–13
   changing of, 8, 9, 10, 11,
   101–103
   and financial mistakes,
   26. *See also* Financial
   mistakes
   guidelines for, 11
   influences on, 9, 10, 12
Statements, 25. *See also*
   Bank statements

Student loans, 65, 67

Tax returns, 23
Transactions
   fees of, 41. *See also*
   Service charges
   recording of, 23, 42,
   44–45, 48, 49–50,
   52. *See also* Bank
   statements; Check
   registers
   types of, 23. *See also*
   specific types
Transportation, costs of,
   107

Unexpected expenses,
   110–115
   debt from, 66, 111
   payment plans for,
   111–115
   saving for, 19. *See also*
   Saving money

Wants. *See* Needs vs.
   wants
Warranties, 110, 113
Web sites
   with budget tools, 93,
   103
   for money management
   courses, 102
Withdrawal slips, 22. *See
   also* Withdrawals
Withdrawals, recording of,
   22, 42, 45